Wildness Unafraid

Wildness Unafraid

Poems by

Tim Murphy

Cover image by Sam Zimmerman / Zhaawanoogiizhik (2024)
Instagram: @cranesuperior
Vector of bird by Deep on Unsplash
Author photo by Tim Murphy

ISBN: 979-8-90146-806-7
Library of Congress Control Number: 2026931902

Kelsay Books
502 South 1040 East, A-119
American Fork, Utah 84003
Kelsaybooks.com

For Ashley, Buttons, and Boris,
and for the wild lands
and their many precious inhabitants.

Acknowledgments

Poems in this volume first appeared in the following publications:

Bed Zine: “Severed”

CERASUS Magazine: “What Crows Think of Us”

Epistemic Literary: “Desert Racers”

Eunoia Review: “City Crickets”

Honeyguide Literary Magazine: “The Hunt”

Livina Press: “Snow Geese Rise”

Louisiana Literature: “Of Cranes and Smoke”

The Orchards Poetry Journal: “Old Oaks”

Remington Review: “Singing Down the Sun”

Reverie Magazine: “Mirage of Stillness”

Sage Magazine: “More Than Just Us”

Tiger Moth Review: “Broken-Winged Heron”

Writers Resist: “Wildness Unafraid”

Contents

What would the trees say about us?
What books would they write
if they had to cut us down?

—Raymond Antrobus, from the poem
"With Birds You're Never Lonely"

Prologue

These poems are remembrances of the living earth. Since falling ill, I often feel severed from the natural environment around me. I miss the vast open space of wilderness, being in another creature's home, seeing a different, slower way of life. Being bedbound has shifted how I relate to nature. It's changed from a daily, direct sensory experience to an occasional glimpse out my window at a bird, a squirrel, or a butterfly. While it carries immense loss and pain, it has made me more attuned to the shifting shadows of clouds, adrift birdsong, to the whispered echoes of rain and wind. Through memory, these poems help me access again, in my mind's eye, the natural world. They serve as reminders that everyone, no matter their circumstance, belongs to the same earth—and that we are all are intertwined with its fate.

As capitalism continues to wage its shameless ecocide at the expense of countless lives, these poems seek to center the plants and animals we live beside but so often forget. They look to other beings for lessons, to remind us that we too are still part of this world. We've grown so estranged, even afraid, of our innate wildness. Yet it's in our recognition of how much we share with nature's other inhabitants, and our leaning into the sense of wonder that nature brings, that we can find a way towards a more sustainable future.

The climate crisis and mass extinctions have long been underway—the consequences of colonialism's relentless violence and greed. We cannot bring back all that we so hastily discarded. But we can learn from the past, which can illuminate what must be done to move beyond the fear of what's coming. Because the fear is very real and justified. Yet how do we dream and believe in a world beyond it? How do we tell stories of all that is left, of all that is at stake? How do live in harmony with other beings? How do we pause before speaking and move more gently through the world? There are no simple answers, of course. But we must start by dreaming that another way is possible and imagining what that world might look like.

—Tim Murphy

Wildness Unafraid

What if trees could talk?
No. Of course they do.
What if we could hear
roots speak
just beneath our feet?

What if birds who lift
the sky with song,
frame it with flight
told us
what names to call them?

What if we simply bathed
in wonder at the coyote's
wild music of the night,
not needing to demonize
to feel alive?

What if we listened deeply,
heeding ancient wisdom
of the many worlds unknown
contained in this one
we don't own?

What if we let other beings
live alongside us
outside the long, lonely shadows
cast by our fear
of our own wildness?

Always Near

The jay's deep blue wing flashes
from just beyond the window.
Bushtits, olives on toothpicks, float
gently down from spindly branches,
swarm and peck the suet feeder, until
a chickadee shoos them away.

Silence, lifted by a nasally horn,
the nuthatch's distant call feels
close yet far, almost melancholy,
summoning a hunger for days gone by.
The finches' cheeping wanders
above unseen in nearby trees.

I was lost in a faraway thought
I will never remember, until
this outer world gently stirred
me back, reminding me
of the many lives beyond our own
always unfolding, always near.

The Hunt

The heron wades slow
silent in shallows
waits patiently, perfectly still.

To a fish, their legs
appear mere sticks
not a spear looming.

Stillness reveals
motion below
their eyes fix wide

crooked neck coils
snaps
pierces water's edge.

And the fish
is no more,
and the heron is fed.

Old Oaks

Blue jays bury
thousands of acorns each fall
all within a mile of the mother tree
only remember where they hid one out of four.

The wide umbrella
deep shade of old oaks
born on wings whose slip of memory
sows seeds that grow well beyond their time.

What Crows Think of Us

Do you ever think about
what other animals must say
behind our back?
Or maybe to our face,
for they know we don't listen
to anyone but ourselves,
and hardly even then.

But let's take Crows. They nose through
our trash, take our shiny things,
live amongst us, know us well.
They must think it odd we need
studies to know they know us.
They must find us aloof. No.
Arrogant. These glorified primates
who need clothes to be seen,
pave the world to stone,
leave the stove of this planet on,
sleepwalk through streets
only noticing our own,
and all the while, still thinking
we are the ones aware.

Perched on a lamppost,
the crow sees us coming.
Reads us like books they don't need.
Walnut in their beak, at the ready.
Drop it just as we draw near,
as we drive on by,
as they feast using these tools
they make of us.

Singing Down the Sun

Dusk descends on the
high desert wetlands.
Coral and fuchsia alight
sun-painted sky
to the west above
a distant, snowy ridge.

Velvety lavender
glows, melts low on the
eastern horizon
framing golden fields
that stretch beyond sight
and the moon's rising.

Red-winged blackbirds
hundreds of them
down by the slough
perch atop cattails
line a telephone pole wire
singing down the sun.

Reaching for One Another

A volcanic tuft ring rises
from a sea of sagebrush
deep in the high desert. No people
nor buildings for miles around. No shrapnel
of our noise that cuts so many silences.
Only the occasional honking calls
of ravens riding waves of wind.

The rocky ring appears as if shaved from atop
an old volcano, its crown placed upon
the desert floor. Millions of years ago,
gentle ripples of a vast lake lapped its walls,
now speckled with wind and water born
alcoves, homes to countless creatures.

In the highest crevices, falcons and swifts nest.
In others, wood rats have lived continuously
for millennia. Generation after generation, they passed
down the exact same nest, in which they rested, ate,
mingled, raised families. Mere holes in a rocky wall
their ancestors came upon thousands of years ago,
through the long stretch of time, these rats, reaching
for one another, forming lasting homes, needing
only each other and their modest nooks, living
off the desert's hidden bounties. The simplicity
of their existence, their hardened, timeless beauty.

City Crickets

Does the cricket know
how many they console
in serenades
not written for our ears?

In a world brimming
with our many lifeless things
droning, numbing sounds
maybe sometimes

hearing someone
else's aliveness
finds again our own
reminds us we're not alone.

Mirage of Stillness

Silence broken by raven wingbeats.
The valley appears empty, still
until coyote's long shadow
traces the distant hillside
as dusk descends.

Rattlesnake awakes, emerges,
squirrel darts through clearing,
the ant's six legs
ever questing.

Rabbits, quail graze,
scurry under sagebrush
almost unseen
by the great owl
whose five-note call
all but freezes
always moving
desert floor.

What Trees Remember

Light softly filters through
the high redwood canopy, appearing
at once bright and shaded. Its own
realm, luminous as a dream's
vision memory holds close.

Ancients, imposing yet inviting, stretch
to the sky beyond the reach of sight.
A nurse log, school buses parked
in a line, donning a thick, layered
sweater spun from moss.

Ferns glow verdant, only broken
by the sliver of a whispered stream.
Fallen cerise-tan needles form the carpet
on which one walks through time
older than our many wars.

Younger trees gleam silver,
still hundreds of years old.
The elders, a deep reddish-brown,
their fibrous, pithy bark, spongy to the touch,
guards from fire, helpless against saws.

Warping scale and space, they usher
in another dimension of their making.
Amidst sentient spirits, bemused
in wonder, I imagine what must hum
softly beneath my feet.

Shallow roots mingling in slow, hushed
tones through fungi-woven webs.
A community sharing
resources, warnings, voicing needs,
collective defense by giving what they can.

In this now rare grove, I envision
the many forests that were like this one
and yet were completely their own, places we stole,
countless creatures stripped from their homes
that became but an object of our covetous desire.

I breathe in their sweetness and earthy
undertones, and a knowing grows
in me: wise trees must know,
when they see us, those we fell,
the timeless we rendered ephemeral.

Desert Racers

High desert
sagebrush
country

first time
I saw
pronghorn run

first time
I saw
wingless flight.

Let Song Dogs Sing

Coyotes vanish in misled crosshairs.
Their fixed gaze not the knife
we sharpen
but a mirror.

Their song, a respite and a threat,
free spirits beyond control.
We extinguish what we won't let
alight within.

But when you see them now,
walking through woods
or down your street,
painting jaw, sagging tongue,
narrow, sly gait

do you not too see
the dog we love
so much
we say we own?

Snow Geese Rise

Content of dreams
from better days.
Walking beneath the sun
in a high desert oasis
one early spring morning.
The cold still clings
to bones and the land.

Sage brush runs
for miles to the east.
A long-armed
fault block mountain
reaches beyond sight
to the west, frames
a vast azure lake.

I pan the water's edge
scan the middle.
A white floating mass
crawling slowly in place
until a glittering mirage
alights my vision
snow drifting upwards
to its origin sky.

As the geese rise
many cries, one echo
through the landscape.
They approach
where I stand
and witness
as they render
a still, blue sky
white and moving.

Forests Robbed for the Trees

When I see the forests we robbed for the trees,
stump-riddled graveyards, the earth left mangled,
I think that the trees were as alive as we are,
that they were another being's home,
before we claimed them as our own.

I think of the doug-firs that stood for centuries,
until we sawed them to pieces, sanded, finished smooth,
laid them down to walk all over.
Even in the tree's death, they could not escape
our ever-stomping feet.

I think of the Chickadee hatchlings,
who nested in the tree that came thundering down,
who lived their very few days sheltered in a nook,
who will never know the joy that must be flight,
who died in the home they were born to leave.

I think of the beetles,
scuttling up the mighty trunk,
crawling along the wavy, deep-grooved bark,
who did not survive the explosion
of their giant tree crashing down
upon the forest floor.

When I see the forests we robbed for the trees,
I cannot unsee, in my own home made of wood,
the dozens of trees that comprise it,
the countless lives swallowed by its walls,
the many deaths on which my life now rests.

Mountain Bluebird

A flicker of radiant
light blue dots
juniper trees.

Wings, a blue
the shade of
tropical seas

flies through
sage that runs
for miles.

Shallow sea blue
glistens across
waterless land.

Rooted

What does the soul need
in a world moving faster
than meaning seems to bloom?
Maybe it’s to live like the tree
in winter, rooted and bare
yet composed within itself,
unhurried, unbothered, waiting,
not grasping beyond the reach
of its delicate branches, nor straining
for things not actually here,
instead merely gathering
fallen water and leaves
that in time feed. Hold dear
all that draws the heart near.

Severed

Exiled
by a living
death disease,
to a bed
where trees
go unseen,
waves of wind
unfelt,
birdsong
unheard.

Even silence rings
in my ears
like howling
grief echoes
in this cave
so dark
I mistake
its walls
for skin.

Broken-Winged Heron

At a small, wooded pond
near where I live dwells
a broken-winged heron.
He does not exist
to inspire wonder,
though wonder
he inspires.

He possesses only himself,
not pushing parts away
to be whole or belong
to something larger,
for only one species insists
disability must be fixed
or assigned perpetual shame.

No, the heron does not write
dreams in the night
of his wing mended
but of the hunt that feeds him,
comforts of nest that hold him,
dangers he must ever know
that breathe him into being.

Encased in these walls,
I still dream of that heron,
still hope we meet again
someday, must believe
the beautiful creature is still
alive, as well as one can be
amidst unsettling times.

What the Land Knows

So many endangered species.
Can we save them?
Can we save them
from the parts of ourselves
that endanger them,
the parts taught
that this world
is here only for us,
other creatures
at the behest
of our hunger, our fear?

Can we see them?
Can we see animals
not merely as equals
but ancient wisdom keepers
essential and belonging
to the land we think we own
treat as dead

the land
whose boundless mystery
sees with many eyes
the many wounds
we've inflicted,
the land
as alive
more aware of
what is coming
than you, than I?

More Than Just Us

A hawk collided with a building
encroaching their wetlands
and broke their shoulder.

They were taken in
and with time and care
their shoulder healed.

The hawk was to be released
at the urban pond where
found injured.

Dozens of us gathered
on a clear mid-autumn day.
They brought the bird over

in a crate, said a few words
about their story, fragments
known of their story.

The crate door opened.
A few tepid steps, wings
arched, spread wide.

The hawk became air
once more, rose to the tree line,
disappeared behind it.

I think often of that bird,
of the many like them
who don't survive

our attempted
severance of self
from the earth

we all belong to.
I think of the many
cages we forge

from beauty
that ensnare
more than just us.

Rodent Kings

Kings of the
urban, rural, and suburban,
the reign of squirrels knows
all domains. Powerhouses
of the rodent world,
their focus, sharper
than hawk talons
they evade.

Always in a hurry,
yet never missing
what they seek.
Running full speed
across fences, along
power lines coursing
through them. Leaping
fearlessly, distant branches
sway without snapping.
Reckless but in control.

Harpoon Fragments

Fragments of harpoons
dated to the 19th century
have been found in living
Bowhead whales.
Earth's oldest mammal,
living over 200 years.
In one, the tip lodged
in their shoulder for centuries.

Our pain buried in them,
forced them to carry longer
than the life of their wounder,
yet outlived by colonial regimes
that set loose the hunter,
that reduced a boundless earth
full of beauty and wonder
to the grasping confines of certainty,
discarding, extracting lives at will,
losing our humanity to feed
wealth that bleeds.

These whales, like all beings,
their radiance their own,
don't exist for us plunder
then centuries later ponder
lessons we don't learn so repeat.
Their ancient, marbled eyes hold open
portals of our timeless violence.

Touched by a Tree

When you touch a tree,
do they not touch you?

Does their ridged bark not ripple
almost imperceptibly across your hand,
does something deeper in them not stir?

Does their immovable immensity,
their disciplined stillness, not move
something in you?

Does the wise tree, who knows
when a storm draws near, see
us as one?

Do we see trees as less than alive
to deaden our conscience
as we cut?

A Fool's Errand

Birdwatching in the high desert,
I came across a fellow birder.
He said there was an owl
in a barn I passed by
minutes earlier.
He said if I went back
I couldn't miss them.

So I walked back to the old barn.
Its wind-battered roof, tattered
in places but mostly intact.
I walked in and looked
up at the wood-beams,
searched every corner,
scanned every wall.
For several minutes
I sought the owl
but their presence
remained a mystery.

At last, before leaving,
my desperation getting
the best of me, I tried to mimic
the owl's call, thinking somehow
it would confuse
my muffled, hideous sound
as its own.

Upon hearing no reply,
almost resigned to leave,
standing in the middle
of the barn, I suddenly felt
a presence and looked
straight up to find
darting back at me
two sharp, dark wide open
eyes. The great horned owl
stared right through me.
The intensity of their gaze
startled me, but I couldn't
look away. For seconds I remember
as minutes, I saw through
their windows a world
far beyond my knowing.

When I came back from the trance
they had me in, suddenly realizing
it was probably best not to stare
any longer at the powerful creature,
I bid them farewell
with a slight bow and left the barn.

The sun shinning outside,
me, smiling, I thought
I had just seen
the first god
I believed in.
And then
I thought
what a fool
the owl must've
thought I was.

On Extinction

Extinction comes from
the Latin word
extinctio
meaning
annihilation,
to extinguish.

As if its root
was a *thing,*
a cataclysmic state
rarely reached
that grew into
an *act* we play out each day

through violence
against
the original peoples
and animals who lived
here first, and against
the land itself.

Because if extinction
is only an ending
we mourn,
not something
we see
ourselves doing,

there will only be more endings,
wolves our fear
hunts down
will only be grieved
once we no longer can see them
breathing, living alongside us,

songbirds straining
to breathe in
our poisoned skies
will be grounded
before we hear their songs
become cries.

Have We Not Killed Enough?

Hunting funds, becomes
many wild places.
Coyote killing contests,
men who need to end a life
to feel their own.
Keep just enough alive
so there will always
be more to kill.

If Birds Could Vote

Who would they make pay
for the half of them missing?
What would their mourning songs say
of the remnant bones of our hunger,
of the wounds we won't tend that cut
new ones and bleed more than just us?

Songs of Blood Memory

Birds each dawn lift the sun with song,
a wild orchestra needs no script
nor conductor, their music simply ebbs
like ripples set moving by the wading heron,
sung from the same strain of blood memory
that's rung through these wetlands for millennia.

Layered voices sound into the valley and beyond.
Red-winged blackbirds perched atop cattails,
and dwindling numbers, warblers, kinglets,
vireos, wrens, migrate great distances,
traverse smokey skies and flashing lights,
struggle to survive the colonizer's ever-reaching
arms, the grasp of the original invasive species.

Still they sing each day to greet
and bid farewell the sun.
But I can't help but wonder:
how many more timeless songs
will we fade to eternal silences,
how many melodies meant to play on
have we already forever turned off?

Crow Funeral

Taking out the trash one morning,
I see a mound of black feathers
and a sharp beak pointed downwards,
claws limp on the ground,
in the grass just by the street.
Above them, a telephone pole wire.

On the ground, surrounding
the fallen bird, a dozen or so crows
all cawing loudly, calling
with their whole bodies bobbing,
a cacophony of sound
spiraling upwards.
I stood transfixed.

Unsure what I was witnessing
I came to sense my presence
may be a disturbance.
After a few moments,
I let them be. And I thought
to myself as I walked
slowly away, that at least
even in death,
the fallen crow
was not alone.

The Tulip Tree

There was an old tulip tree
in the front yard of my former home.
Their majestic canopy rose far above
the other city trees, except for another
tulip tree just yards away
on our neighbor's lot, they rose
to meet each other's eyeline.

I would often sit and close my eyes
under the great tree, feel its shade cool
my skin, slow my thoughts. I would close
my eyes and listen
to the soft whir of breeze threading
through thick, wide, leathery leaves.
And for a moment, all else seemed to cease.

I hope that tree and its companion outlive me.
I hope others receive the same comfort
they afforded me, and I hope we never tear down
beings who can lift even heavy spirits.

Delicate Survival

Butterflies weigh half a paperclip but floated
alongside dinosaurs, survived asteroids
and ice ages giants and mammoths could not.

They weathered waves of wind across great seas,
furthest reaches of the arctic, nearly every continent
in between, withstood vulnerabilities of delicate wings
raindrops pierce. Storms that throw them from
blood memory's trail. Their lives, only weeks for some,
links in a chain that endures the long stretch of time itself.

Wired for millennia, knowing when to leave,
where to stop, all mangled by our sea of pesticides
spread casually, our mingling that set the oven
of the sun on far too long, the effects only starting
to cascade, to confuse plants into flowering
too early or too late. A gamble we've made
of once steady seasons. These seemingly frail
yet lasting creatures survived so much,
but will they, in the end, survive us?

Of Cranes and Smoke

One early autumn morning,
I am driving through
a vast river island,
where each fall, thousands
of migratory birds gather.
Azure sky frames
yellowing cottonwoods.

I drive until road's end,
a golden prairie bordered
by a distant, shallow lake.
Silence I anticipate fills
with a loud bugle call,
answered by many more,
fast approaching from behind.

Feather-tipped wings
fill my vision, hundreds
of sandhill cranes pass
low overheard, rolling
primordial cries echo
through the landscape
and I hear nothing else.

The cranes near the lake,
whirl downwards in soft circles,
dangle legs like landing gears,
bodies splayed and still until
mere feet from the ground,
great wings beat upwards and
they land with grace and ease.

I watch the cranes
the rest of the morning,
as they feed in long grasses,
leap whimsically in shallows.
In their presence, I feel young
and old and time escapes me.

Yet only for brief moments
could I forget the preceding weeks
of sorrow, of ash and smoke-filled sky
that singed lungs forced to breathe it.
And I can’t help but think
of the cranes unseen before me,
who made the trek alongside their kin,
not knowing it would be their last.

I think of the maps stitched
in the crane's mind at birth
passed through generations
of blood memory
that allow them to navigate
the vast ocean of the darkest sky
by following the stars within it,

maps that for millennia
showed them the way home
no matter the distance
but which I fear cannot bridge
this widening divide
between the earth we were given
and the one we plunder
with our self-filled vision.

I look to the cranes as I go.
A silent plea grows in me:
before more forever lost
we see, each radiant being
a sacred presence
whose absence leaves
a hole one cannot fill
in this living, burning,
still breathing earth.

About the Author

Tim Murphy is a disabled poet from Portland, Oregon. His writing explores chronic illness, disability justice, and our complex, tenuous relationship to the more-than-human world. Tim is bedbound with Long COVID and severe Myalgic Enceph-alomyelitis (ME). By writing about the natural world, it helps him access, through memory, the wild places that have touched his life. Tim's poetry appears in *Louisiana Literature, Kaleidoscope, Wordgathering, The Sunlight Press,* and more.

Instagram and Bluesky:
@brokenwingpoet

www.ingramcontent.com/pod-product-compliance
Lightning Source LLC
LaVergne TN
LVHW050610100826
845148LV00015B/3209